MARKETING RESEARCH AND THE BOTTOM OF THE PYRAMID: A STUDY ANALYSIS

DR. CHANTELL BEATY

Dr. Beaty is a Doctor of Business Administration (DBA) – with special reference to International Business and Marketing at Walden University, Minneapolis, Minnesota, United States. A certified researcher and Bottom of the Pyramid (BOP) economic specialist with extensive research and study in BOP markets. Doctoral research study: Business Leaders Marketing to Bottom of the Pyramid Consumers of Nigeria. Dr. Beaty has over 25 years in business administration. Dr. Beaty's careers include an extensive profile of experience with the United States Federal Government, GSA; Department of Homeland Security, FEMA (Unsung Heroes Award); and Department of Defense, United States Air Force, civilian duty. Dr. Beaty's background in education extends from teaching at the local college to teaching as a certified math teacher in a range of grades from elementary to high school, special education to gifted and talented, and now managing her own start up University for business leaders of the world. Dr. Beaty's business ownership background covers a broad range of business knowledge and ownership from sales director to international researcher and consultant. Dr. Beaty is an International Gold Key Scholar, and holds a Bachelor's of Science (BS) and Masters of Business Administration (MBA) from Texas Wesleyan University.

C.R. Beaty & Associates

www.ChantellBeaty.com

Marketing Research and the Bottom of the Pyramid: A Study Analysis

Chantell Beaty

Abstract

Marketing research and marketing strategies are terms used to insight marketers for managing products and services domestically and globally while catering to the needs of consumers. There are various trends and innovations in marketing research. Marketing researchers reveal gaps in the literature and the need for continued research. Customer resource management and technology is a trending aspect of marketing research and leads to the enhancement of organization based on further research and studies. The researcher presents a background, analysis of the field and future contribution to marketing research in terms of the bottom of the pyramid marketing and research.

Table of Contents

Marketing Research and the Bottom of the Pyramid

Performing marketing research at the bottom of the economic pyramid is one way to assist business leaders in developing marketing strategies to market to Nigerian consumers and consumers in emerging economies. A qualitative study with a case study design may demonstrate the potential for marketing researchers to contribute to the concerns of business owners expanding their corporate strategy to emerging economies with concentrated populations at the base of the economic pyramid. This study and analysis may provide viable information for business leaders and researchers in the field of marketing research.

Critical Analysis and Synthesis of the Literature

I began the research with an analysis of the field of marketing research. Areas such as classical research versus modern research, trends and innovations in marketing research, and current topics in marketing research were contributing information to my analysis. Furthermore, I addressed the field of marketing as it pertained to the bottom of the pyramid (BOP). Also, I addressed the concept of BOP marketing theory along with opposing and supporting theories of this concept. Finally, I demonstrated a presentation of the findings for future directions in marketing research.

Analysis of the Field of Marketing Research

Researchers in marketing research still follow the scientific method. Although some companies seek out qualitative methods to clarify consumer experiences (Belk, 2006); few studies are available that include insight into the selection, implementation, and development of appropriate qualitative methods by specific companies (Sunderland & Denny, 2007). A review of research methods used in marketing reveals that quantitative methods continue to dominate (Hewege & Perera, 2013). Only, recently have marketing scientist become concerned with issues in philosophy (Deshpande, 1983). Almost three decades ago the overreliance on quantitative methods in academic research was realized, consequently the need for alternative research methods raised (Deshpande, 1983).

An effective method for conducting a marketing research study is through research triangulation or mixed method. Hewege and Perera (2013) discussed that many marketing researchers have argued that there is a need for resolving the problem of overreliance on quantitative research methods and for moving towards the combined use of both methods for researchers to understand this marketing phenomenon. In addition, according to their research, other researchers suggests that qualitative research methods such as in-depth interviews, participant observations, ethnography, and others are not common in academic marketing research (Hewege & Perera, 2013). Instead, the use of research methods such as experiments, surveys, and other hypotheticodeductive, quantitative methods are common (Hewege & Perera, 2013). Marketing researchers tend to borrow models, tools, and techniques from other sciences, such as statistics and economics (Carroll & Green, 1995).

Classical versus Modern

In terms of classical research compared to modern research, researchers in marketing research have opportunities to contribute to the field with various types of methods, designs, and new information. Researchers such as Holt (1991) discussed both the need for providing objective evaluation criteria when using naturalistic research techniques and the limitations of trying to create an objective test for subjective insights. Also, researchers have the opportunity to integrate humanistic inquiry into marketing research and propose ways in which to accomplish this (Hirschman, 1986). Furthermore, in terms of research such as case research, Bonoma (1985) argued that case research is a useful tool for expanding insights gained into complex phenomena in the field. In the interest of developing marketing strategies, Shih (1986) developed a system whereby researchers could recommend changes in marketing strategies and target markets. Finally, Golafshani (2003) defined reliability and validity in qualitative research whereby reliability and validity were two standards of scientific research that often associated with the quantitative methods.

Trends and Innovations

Understanding consumer behavior is very crucial in making right marketing decisions, and marketing research have been evolving to provide marketers with this information in the most reliable way. Deutskens, De Ruyter, and Wetzels (2006) compared the quality of surveys taken online and through the mail, as well as common types of feedback given in each format. As far as the value of online surveys, Evans and Mather (2005) presented an in-depth look at the advantages and disadvantages of online surveys and provided additional insight into current trends in online research. Roster, Rogers, Albaum, and Klein (2004) compared the quality of responses and responsiveness in the web and telephone surveys, as well as the costs associated with both approaches. As customer satisfaction, customer loyalty and marketing research in

6

general relied on tracking studies, the internet provided market researchers significant cost-effective means of recruiting respondents and using online research tools to maintain and develop customer relationships (Fulgoni, 2014). Researchers relied on relationship marketing (RM) strategy to disclose detailed information in terms of the importance given by consumers to certain aspects related to products and services (Constantin, 2014). In turn, such researchers measured the performance of organizations in delivering those products and services that met or exceeded the customers' expectations (Constantin, 2014).

Current Topics in Marketing Research

Shaw, Subramanian, Tan, & Welge (2001) presented their views on knowledge management and data mining for marketing. The authors discussed applying some of the data mining and knowledge management applications and practices that were common in other functions to the marketing function, thereby providing a means to support marketing managers' decision-making. RDE is a systemized business process of experimentation that enables the business to design, test, and modify alternative products or services. Rule developing experimentation RDE empowered businesses with the knowledge that appealed to the customer, even if the customer does not know within competitive environments.

Selling Blue Elephants is a compendium of examples showing how such companies as Hewlett-Packard, Maxwell House, Vlasic, Prego, MasterCard, Kay Jewelers, and Abacus Electronics have used conjoint measurement (Moskowitz & Gofman, 2007). The authors introduced their rule developing experimentation (RDE) methodology and provided detailed descriptions of how researchers used this approach to identify promotional "hot button messages" and devised new products and strategies (Moskowitz & Gofman, 2007).

Conjoint analysis (discrete choice estimation or stated preference research) is an innovative market research technique that uncovered how people made decisions and perceived their value in products and services (Moskowitz & Gofman, 2007). The conjoint analysis involved presenting people with choices and then analyzing the drivers for those choices (Moskowitz & Gofman, 2007). Researchers can quantify the hidden rules people use to make trade-offs between different products and services (Moskowitz & Gofman, 2007). Likewise, researchers can further quantify the values they place on different features or parts of the offer (Moskowitz & Gofman, 2007).

Market segmentation is when business leaders focus on the behaviors and buying habits of consumers (Martin. 2011). Marketing research and business leaders must think for organizations innovatively to be successful in today's global market (Martin, 2011). Martin (2011) suggested that researchers and organization leaders adapt to new ways of doing business and use the correct business segmentation strategy. Such innovation would include RDE and conjoint analysis. Therefore, marketing segmentation by business leaders provided an advantage in business strategies with trust-based segmentation (Dimitriadis, Kouremenos & Kyrezis, 2011); and thereby contribute to the profitability of business leaders marketing to consumers at the base/bottom of the economic pyramid (BOP) (Prahalad, 2005).

The Future of Marketing Research

As organizations adopted customer relationship management (CRM), centered on the customer to cope with recent technological change and new digital strategy, more research is viable via people-centric approaches (Bernoff & Li, 2008). Therefore, relevant research is necessary to present strategic direction for successful CRM development as the digital era keeps on evolving (Quinton, 2013). There is no specific research on relationship marketing (RM) that focuses on the generation Y market. Also, organizations need to focus on new consumer market segments in a more determined manner and building strong relationships with them in the long term (Mirpuri & Narwani, 2012).

Literature regarding online surveys compared to mail surveys was evident. However, empirical research that contracted actual respondent behavior to online surveys, with actual respondent behavior to mail surveys was limited (Evans & Marthur, 2005). Most of the academic research with respect to online marketing research resulted in countries such as the United States (US) and the United Kingdom (UK). In these areas internet penetration was high. Therefore, there need to be studies conducted with respect to countries with lower internet penetration in order for researchers to understand the response rate and its usefulness (Deutskens, Ruyter & Wetzels, 2006). Furthermore, online marketing research is popular in the case of business consumers. However, slight research resulted in finding the effectiveness of online marketing research with respect to consumers as end-users.

Interpreting and analyzing data collected from online surveys appeared to be more of an art than science. This requires further probing. There were various results in terms of the reliability of data collected online. It is important to have more in-depth empirical studies that prove the reliability and validity of such online data for use without any doubt. If reliability, validity, and triangulation, are to be relevant research concepts, from a qualitative point of view, researchers will have to redefine these concepts in order to reflect multiple ways of establishing truth (Golafshani, 2003).

Moreover, businesses are not utilizing social media practices for B2B relationships (Jussila, Kärkkäinen, & Aramo-Immonen, 2014). This is because of the inability of firms to assess its benefits and measurement of ROI (Jussila, Kärkkäinen, & Aramo-Immonen, 2014). Also, regarding business to consumer relationships (B2C), a gap exists in the literature about researchers understanding of the market segment relating to RDE and conjoint analysis. Segmentation plays a critical role in RDE and conjoint analysis. The process of segmentation begins with research and market analysis to identify key segments. Business success depends on implementing a segmentation strategy that involves aligning the organization to deliver appropriately for each consumer segment. Trust-based segmentation proved to be meaningful in terms of businesses determining behavioral intentions. Manipulation of behavioral intentions to inform and educate customers on the Internet, and mobile platforms was proven to be a low cost - high-efficiency means, as compared to mass media above the line (ATL) advertising (Dimitriadis, Kouremenos & Kyrezis, 2011). However, this type of segmentation relied on consumer trust in companies and their trust in its technology channels (Dimitriadis, Kouremenos & Kyrezis, 2011). Finally, since segmentation has not exhausted in industry markets, Reid and

Plank (2000) suggested the use of more programmatic research techniques utilizing technology databases.

Example of a Qualitative Research Topic: Marketing Research and the Bottom of the Pyramid

The purpose of this qualitative case study was to explore how some business leaders develop marketing strategies that help them market to Nigerian consumers. The targeted population comprised of business owners in the South Central region of the United States who market to consumers in Nigeria, and who have successfully developed strategies that help them market to Nigerian consumers. The implications for positive social change include the potential for business leaders to share best practice business strategies to market to Nigerian consumers, and possibly create entrepreneurship and job opportunities for Nigerian communities.

The bottom of the pyramid (BOP) market consists of over four billion people who live on less than $2/day (Prahalad, 2012). However, the four billion people who make up the BOP are not a monolith (Prahalad, 2012). They represent multiple cultures, ethnicity, literacy, capabilities, and needs and a segment in multiple ways (Prahalad, 2012). According to the International Finance Corporation (IFC) and the World Bank group, the four billion people at the base of the economic pyramid (BOP) live in relative poverty and have incomes below $3,000 in local purchasing power, yet their economic potential is significant (International Finance Corporation, 2015). Furthermore, across countries such as Latin America, 70 percent of the population lives at the BOP and that number increases to 75 percent in Brazil and Mexico. This represents a $509 billion untapped market, and IFC's strategy seeks to reach these underserved millions by fostering an inclusive market-based approach (International Finance Corporation World Bank Group, 2015).

Chikweche and Fletcher (2012) examined qualitative issues involved in conducting research at the base of the pyramid (BOP). Their qualitative data collection methods comprised of in-depth one to one consumer interviews, focus groups, ethnographic observations and case studies to conduct the research. Research into the BOP is a relatively new area of study in international business, and, therefore, there is a limited amount of previous literature on this topic (Chikweche & Fletcher, 2012). Chikweche and Fletcher used qualitative methods to identify the challenges faced by researchers when conducting research at the BOP. They demonstrated how this approach was particularly relevant at the BOP because it captured the nuances and challenges of studying BOP consumers in their real life situations and observing them participating in activities. This provided Chikweche and Fletcher with insights into the behavior of these consumers and their attitude towards being the subject of research. By so doing, they were able to understand the complex meaning of specific actions and beliefs, thereby addressing the *why* and *how* aspects of conducting research at the BOP. The BOP market is not a monolith (Prahalad, 2012); however, according to Chikweche and Fletcher, the reference in previous studies was only in reference to developing country markets where researchers treated the market primarily as a homogenous entity.

The bottom of the pyramid (BOP) markets is a new source of radical innovation (Prahalad, 2012). By focusing managerial attention on creating awareness, access, affordability, and availability, the 4As of marketing as opposed to price, product, promotion, and place, the 4Ps of marketing, managers can create an exciting environment for innovation (Prahalad, 2012). BOP markets by definition demand new services and applications, and, as a result, BOP markets can be a source of new developments (Prahalad, 2012). Therefore, there are particular industries, such as the wireless industry and banking industry, and various technologies such as cell phones and ATMs that the BOP market will influence. This is a positive impact and maximizes by systems thinking as a prerequisite for success in BOP markets.

Although, Prahalad (2012) suggested that recognizing the BOP market, the four billion underserved consumers, as a legitimate market consisting of micro consumers, micro producers, micro investors, and innovators, is the first step to understanding the potential of BOP markets, global firms, and active participation in BOP markets, is not an option. Lessons that global firms learned in BOP markets, such as dramatic changes in price performance (value), use of hybrid technologies, lean management, market development, deskilling of work, collaboration with NGOS and the public sector, and distribution and logistics in hostile conditions, are the qualities that will serve them well in becoming globally competitive (Prahalad, 2012). In effect, according to Prahalad the participation in BOP markets and innovation will set the global competitiveness agenda for the next decade

Critical Analysis and Synthesis of Literature Pertaining to BOP Marketing Theory

In 1998-1999, Prahalad and colleagues introduced the base/bottom of the pyramid (BOP) concept in an article and a working paper (Kolk, Santos, & Rufin, 2012). Although initial aspects of the BOP concept developed in Prahalad's coauthored 1998 article in the *Harvard Business*

Review (Prahalad & Lieberthal, 1998), the first fully elaborated articulation of the BOP concept circulated as a working paper by Prahalad and Hart (1999) dated August 1999 (Kolk, Santos, & Rufin, 2012). Prahalad's original work was a call for the multinational enterprise (MNE) to target BOP markets and thus help alleviate poverty (Prahalad & Hammond, 2002; Prahalad & Lieberthal, 1998). However, Kolk, Santos, and Ruffin, 2012 showed that the original approach evolved drastically over the period of 1999-2009, and MNEs led only a small number of reported BOP initiatives.

Prahalad (2005) later extended his works and the works of his colleagues with a theory that explained the profitability of business leaders marketing to consumers at the base of the economic pyramid. There are four billion people in the world with an annual per capita income based on purchasing-power-parity (PPP) of less than 1,500 dollars. This PPP is a profitable market for businesses (Prahalad, 2005). According to the dominant logic, some business leaders make assumptions and implications that this annual income is low; however, the BOP market concept challenges this view by containing research instructions that permit the researcher to demonstrate to those interested that this market is significant (Prahalad, 2005). Significant tenets or propositions underlying the concept of the BOP market are (a) there is a potential for profit at the BOP (b) there is ready access to BOP markets (c) the BOP markets are brand-conscious (d) the BOP markets are critical factors in worldwide wireless growth, and (e) BOP consumers accept advanced technology readily (Prahalad, 2005).

The BOP market theory is applicable and applies to developing business strategies that market to Nigerian consumers because some business leaders can use the tenets or propositions underlying these concepts to convert the BOP market to a consumer market (Prahalad, 2005). Business leaders can then move towards creating the capacity of the BOP market to a consumer market (Prahalad, 2005). Furthermore, business leaders with an active consumer market at the BOP may not only contribute to how to develop strategies that can help market to Nigerian consumers but may increase the standards of living within the Nigerian communities.

Critical Analysis with Supporting and Contrasting Conceptual Models for BOP Marketing

Over the subsequent years, Kolk, Santos, and Rufin, 2012 found debates have emerged, approaches and definitions have evolved, and the very idea that MNEs should be searching for a fortune at the BOP has been questioned both by proponents of the BOP approach, such as Ted London (London, Hart, & Barney, 2011), and by its critics, such as Karnani (2011). Kolk, Santos, and Rufin, also mentioned De Soto's (2000) work that emphasized the entrepreneurial potential of the poor.

Chikweche and Fletcher (2012) introduced that advocates such as Prahalad and Hart (2002) catering to the BOP market argued that the challenges in serving it do not arise merely from the actual number of people in the market, but lie in need to re-invent Western models of doing business to fit the local requirements of this vast market. In addition, Chikweche and Fletcher stated that in reference to Khanna, Palepu, and Sinha (2005), companies that develop strategies that take into account the unique conditions of the BOP market and do not attempt to serve the market based on Western approaches, are likely to succeed in exploring the potential that exists at the BOP. The BOP market is unlikely to be one huge homogeneous entity, but one that has some segments, each with unique needs and system requirements (Chikweche &

Fletcher, 2012). Furthermore, Chikweche and Fletcher stated that it is necessary for companies to understand this to adapt their business models to facilitate effective engagement with the BOP.

There is an opposing school of thought such as Karnani (2006) and Landrum (2007) that questions the desirability of focusing on the BOP market, pointing to the lack of consensus on classification, the size of the market, and the problems of reducing poverty (Chikweche & Fletcher, 2012). However, Chikweche and Fletcher added, there is a consensus by both advocates and opponents of firm engagement with the BOP such as Landrum on the fact that there will never be agreement on actual size and classification of the market but that it is an important market that requires increased research on its dynamics and the behavior of its consumers.

Comparison and Contrast of Points of View in BOP Marketing Research

The World Resource Institute, International Finance Corporation and World Bank Group (2007) responded to criticisms of the BOP market approach. Gebauer and Reynoso (2013) highlighted the main topics in the emerging BOP debate. Finally, Kolk, Santos, and Rufin (2014) discussed that some main topics in the BOP debate were (a) the definition of BOP markets (b) the role of corporations in BOP markets (c) the size and PPP of BOP markets, and (d) whether at all to market to BOP markets or the poor.

Definition of BOP Markets

Kolk, Santos, and Rufin (2012) conducted a systematic review of articles on the BOP, identifying 104 articles published in journals or proceedings over a 10-year period (2000-

2009). What has become of the concept over the decade following its first systematic exposition in 1999 was the research question (Kolk, Santos & Ruffin, 2012). Kok et al. (2012) answered this question by stating the corporations needed to be particularly clear regarding their definition of the BOP, as variations across BOP contexts were likely to make quick generalizations and discussions that would apply throughout the BOP questionable. Calton, Werhane, Hartman and Bevan (2013) argued in a paper the definition of the BOP in terms of recalibrating a strategic focus by "creating a fortune with the base of the pyramid" rather than at the BOP and coined this as a new shift in the language. The new language shift would counter the original market-based approach of capturing markets rather than enabling new socially entrepreneurial ventures for BOP consumers otherwise trapped in conditions of extreme poverty.

Role of Corporations in BOP Markets

The findings of the Kolk, Santos, and Ruffin's (2012) BOP review of a decade of articles from 2000 to 2009 resulted in additional information to Prahalad's (2005) and collaborators' (Prahalad & Hammond, 2002; Prahalad & Hart, 1999; Prahalad & Lieberthal, 1998) original idea that large MNEs had a central role to play in BOP marketing. Kolk et al. (2012) found that MNEs led only a small number of reported BOP initiatives. Therefore, BOP scholars (Prahalad, 2005, 2012, 2014; Prahalad & Hammond, 2002; Prahalad & Hart, 1999; Prahalad & Lieberthal, 1998; Chikweche, 2013; Chikweche & Fletcher, 2012a, 2012b, 2013a, 2013b, Chikweche et al., 2012; Murisa & Chikweche, 2013) actually highlight the important role business leaders' play in BOP marketing. This role is not just by large MNEs, but also by small companies, domestic companies, social entrepreneurs, not-for-profit organizations, and government agencies (Kolk et al., 2012).

Size and Purchasing Power Parity of the BOP Markets

Prahalad and Hart (1999) presented a model of the world economic pyramid with a breakdown of four tiers, with tiers two and three in the middle. The pyramid reflected population and PPP in U.S. dollars. Prahalad and Hart (1999) reflected the thought of the global market as a pyramid. At the very top of the pyramid there existed a small fraction, as a percentage of global population, of customers corresponding to the affluent in developed countries such as the U.S. (Prahalad & Hart, 1999). Then they considered the vast emerging consumer base at the BOP where three to four billion people resided (Prahalad & Hart, 1999). In contrast, the World Resource Institute, International Finance Corporation, and World Bank Group (2007) researchers presented a market size and business strategy at the BOB with a data-driven market analysis for business leaders to analyze all BOP market segments and market sectors of the BOP population. The World Resource Institute, International Finance Corporation, and World Bank Group (2007) researchers presented the primary BOP market segment as those with annual income up to and including $3000 per capita per year per 2002 PPP reports. Gupta and Pirsch (2014) presented an article with 261 respondents arguing that the current size of the BOP market segment was approximately 4 billion people and expected to grow to 6 billion people with $5 trillion in purchasing power over the next 40 years.

Whether at All to Market to BOP Markets

Hemais, Casotti, and Rocha (2013) presented research based in Brazil and discussed how two lines of argument had arisen with distinct perspectives regarding marketing to the BOP. The first argument supported a hedonistic approach, where consumption at the BOP was a wish to reduce poverty, while the other, where a moralistic standpoint was predominant, criticized this view because it argued that people's lives could only improve by including people with less purchasing power in the production processes. Ansari, Munir, and Gregg (2012) believed that business leaders' evaluation of any BOP initiative underpinnings was according to the enhancement of social capital between the community and the ability to preserve the existing social capital in the area.

Gupta and Pirsch (2014) presented a quantitative analysis and a sample size of 261 respondents who answered to an online survey. Based on three varying hypotheses, Gupta and Pirsch (2014) argued that companies could be exploiting the poor through practices such as misleading sales promotion, lack of fair pricing, deceptive advertising, and inappropriateness in the use of products. In addition, Kennedy, Bardy, and Rubens (2012) examined whether there is practical evidence to support the assumption that doing business through FDI improved social conditions in less developed countries and whether the logic for this to happen is rooted in ethical theory. However, Mason, Chakrabarti, and Singh (2013) explained BOP markets in terms of what they were and why they mattered.

Presentation of Findings and Future Directions

In conclusion, there are specific areas of further research in this topic that would prove

beneficial. Overall, the analysis and review lead to a call for precise definitions and explicit

analysis of the characteristics of the BOP initiative discussed in future BOP articles (Kolk,

Santos, & Rufin, 2012). In addition, authors need to be particularly clear regarding their

definition of the BOP, as variations across BOP contexts are likely to make quick generalizations

and discussions that would apply throughout the BOP questionable (Kolk, Santos, & Rufin,

2012). Similarly, the findings of this review show that, contrasting with Prahalad's original idea

that large MNEs had a central role to play in BOP initiatives (Prahalad & Hammond, 2002;

Prahalad & Lieberthal, 1998), only a small number of reported BOP initiatives are led by MNEs

(Kolk, Santos, & Rufin, 2012). Therefore, BOP Scholars have thus highlighted the important role

that can be played not just by large MNEs but also by small companies, domestic companies,

social entrepreneurs, and even not-for-profit organizations and government agencies (Kolk,

Santos, & Rufin, 2012). Thorough discussions of the role of different actors in BOP initiatives

are therefore called for, as these discussions carry important implications for the very notion of

profitability at the BOP (Kolk, Santos, & Rufin, 2012). Finally, as suggested by Kolk, Santos, &

Rufin (2012) many cases and examples originate from Africa, India, and other emerging

economies, and a broadening of the empirical base, seems necessary. (Read more at

www.ChantellBeaty.com/Bookstore, *Business Leaders Marketing to the Bottom of the Pyramid*

Consumers in Nigeria).

Marketing research is important in expanding new and innovative information in research. Quantitative research is common to marketing research; however, researchers are now exploring qualitative cases in research as a means to understanding various aspects of marketing. Marketing to the BOP is an example of a qualitative research topic in marketing. Qualitative research in marketing to the BOP consumers is necessary for capturing this market for business success.

References

Belk, R.W. (2006). *Handbook of qualitative research methods in marketing*, Edward Elgar: Cheltenham, U.K./Northampton, MA.

Bonoma, T. V. (1985). Case research in marketing: Opportunities, problems, and a process. *Journal of Marketing Research*, 22, 199-208. doi.org/10.2307/3151365

Carroll, J. D., & Green, P. E. (1995). Guest editorial: Psychometric methods in marketing research: Part I, conjoint analysis. *Journal of marketing Research*, 32, 385-391. doi: 10.2307/3152174

Chikweche, T. & Fletcher. R. (2012). Undertaking research at the bottom of the pyramid using qualitative methods. Qualitative Market Research: An International Journal, 15, 242–267. doi: 10.1108/13522751211231978

Constantin, C. (2014). Using the importance-satisfaction matrix relationship marketing strategies. *Bulletin of the Transylvania University of Brasov. Series V: Economic Sciences, 7*(1), 31-36. Retrieved from http://webbut.unitbv.ro/

Dimitriadis, S., Kouremenos, A., & Kyrezis, N. (2011). Trust-based segmentation. The International Journal of Bank Marketing,
29(1), 5-31. doi:10.1108/02652321111101356

De Soto, H. (2000). *The mystery of capital: Why capitalism triumphs in the West and fails everywhere else*. New York, NY: Basic Books.

Deutskens, E., De Ruyter, K., & Wetzels, M. (2006). An assessment of equivalence between online and mail surveys in service research. *Journal of Service Research, 8*, 346-355. doi:10.1177/1094670506286323

Evans, J. R., & Mathur, A. (2005). The value of online surveys. *Internet Research, 15*, 195-219. doi:10.1108/10662240510590360

Fulgoni, G. (2014). Uses and misuses of online-survey panels in digital research. *Journal of Advertising Research, 54*(2), 133-137. doi:10.2501/JAR-54-2-133-137c

Golafshani, N. (2003). Understanding reliability and validity in qualitative research. The Quarterly Report, 8, 597-607. Retrieved from http://www.nova.edu/ssss/QR/QR8-4/golafshani

Hewege, C. R., & Perera, L. C. R. (2013). In search of alternative research methods in marketing: Insights from layder's adaptive theory methodology. *Contemporary Management Research*, 9, 343-360. Retrieved from http://www.cmr-journal.org/

Hirschman, E. C. (1986). Humanistic inquiry in marketing research: Philosophy, method, and criteria. *Journal of Marketing Research*, 23, 237–249. doi: 10.2307/3151482

Holt, D. B. (1991). Rashomon visits consumer behavior: An interpretative critique of naturalistic inquiry. *Advances in Consumer Research*, 18, 57–62. Retrieved from http://www.researchgate.net/journal/0098-

International Finance Corporation World Bank Group (2015). *Base of the economic pyramid (BOP)*. Retrieved from http://www.ifc.org/wps/wcm/connect/region__ext_content/regions/latin+america+and+the+caribbean/strategy/base+of+the+economic+pyramid

Jussila, J. J., Kärkkäinen, H., & Aramo-Immonen, H. (2014). Social media utilization in business-to-business relationships of technology industry firms. *Computers in Human Behavior, 30*, 606-613. Retrieved from: http://dl.acm.org/

Khanna, T., Palepu, K. and Sinha, J. (2005), Strategies that fit emerging markets, *Harvard Business Review*, 83(6). 63-76. Retrieved from https://hbr.org/

Karnani, A. (2011). *Fighting poverty together—Rethinking strategies for business, governments, and civil society to reduce poverty.* New York, NY: Palgrave Macmillan.

Landrum, N.E. (2007), Advancing the base of the pyramid debate, *Strategic Management Review. 1(1)*, 1-12. Retrieved from http://www.strategicmanagementreview.com/

London, T., Hart, S., & Barney, J. (2011, August 14). Next generation base of the pyramid strategy. Academy of Management Conference (Session # 420), San Antonio, TX.

Martin, G. (2011). The importance of marketing segmentation. American Journal of Business Education, 3(6), 15-18. Retrieved from http://www.cluteinstitute.com/journals/american-journal-of-business-education-ajbe/

Mirpuri, D. G., & Narwani, S. A. (2012). Measuring relationship quality towards the Generation Y market in the mobile telecommunications industry-An empirical study. *Journal of Services Research*, 2, 57. Retrieved from http://www.jsr-iimt.in/

Moskowitz, H., & Gofman, A. (2007). *Selling blue elephants.* Upper Saddle River, NJ: Wharton School Publishing.

Prahalad, C. K. (2002). Strategies for the bottom of the economic pyramid: India as a source of innovation. *Reflections*, 3(4), 6-17.

Prahalad, C. K. (2005). *The fortune at the bottom of the pyramid: Eradicating poverty through profits*. Upper Saddle River, NJ: Wharton School Publishing.

Prahalad, C. K., & Hart, S. (1999). Strategies for the bottom of the pyramid: Creating sustainable development (Working paper). Ann Arbor: University of Michigan. Retrieved from http://www.bus.tu.ac.th/usr/wai/xm622/conclude%620monsanto/ strategies.pdf

Prahalad, C. K., & Hart, S. L. (2002). The fortune at the bottom of the pyramid. *Strategy+Business*, 20, 1-13. Retrieved from http://www.strategy-business.com/

Prahalad, C. K., & Lieberthal, K. (1998). The end of corporate imperialism. *Harvard Business Review*, 76(4), 68-79. Retrieved from https://hbr.org/

Quinton, S. (2013). The digital era requires new knowledge to develop relevant CRM strategy: A cry for adopting social media research methods to elicit this new knowledge. *Journal of Strategic Marketing, 21*, 402-412. doi:10.1080/0965254X.2013.801611

Reid, D. A., & Plank, R. E. (2000). Business Marketing Comes of Age: A Comprehensive Review of the Literature. Journal of Business-to-Business Marketing, 7, 9–186. doi:10.1300/j033v07n02_02

Roster, C. A., Rogers, R. D., Albaum, G., & Klein, D. (2004). A comparison of response characteristics from web and telephone surveys. *International Journal of Market Research, 46*, 359-374. Retrieved from http://www.ebscohost.com/academic/business-source-complete

Shaw, M. J., Subramaniam, C., Tan, G. W., & Welge, M. E. (2001). Knowledge management

    and data mining for marketing. *Decision Support Systems, 31*, 127-137.

    doi:10.1016/S0167-9236(00)00123-8

Shih, S. (1986). VALS as a tool of tourism market research: The Pennsylvania

    experience. *Journal of Travel Research, 24*, 2-11. doi: 10.1177/004728758602400401

Sunderland, P. & Denny, R. (2007). *Doing anthropology in consumer research.* Left Coast

    Press: Walnut Creek, CA.